CONTENTS

REGULATION
OF AUTOMOBILE
SAFETY

Sam Peltzman

American Enterprise Institute for Public Policy Research
Washington, D. C.

Sam Peltzman is professor of business economics, Graduate School of Business, University of Chicago.

ISBN 0-8447-3194-3

Evaluative Studies 26, December 1975

Library of Congress Catalog Card No. 75-39779

Printed in the United States of America

REGULATION
OF AUTOMOBILE
SAFETY

INTRODUCTION

From 1947 to 1960 the highway death rate, expressed as deaths per vehicle mile, declined by about 3.5 percent per year. In the next five years the death rate rose by about 1 percent per year. Responding to this turnabout, Congress passed in 1966 the National Traffic and Motor Vehicle Safety Act, making it mandatory for each new car to be equipped with devices designed to prevent deaths and injuries to the occupants. From 1966 to 1972, the death rate declined by an annual average of over 3.5 percent, a fact that must have heartened the framers of this act. But can the decline be attributed to the act, or does it merely reflect a resurgence of the forces that were responsible for the decline up to 1960? This is the central question addressed in this study.

Safety regulation has had little or nothing to do with the renewed decline in the death rate. It is not that the required safety devices have failed to do their intended work. They *do* work, but their very efficacy has created forces that in fact have compromised their lifesaving potential.

The first part of this study summarizes the technical literature on the lifesaving potential of the safety devices. The second explains why economic theory suggests that this potential might be overstated. The main part of the study establishes empirically the net effect of auto safety regulation on the highway death rate. Finally, the last section examines the implications of the evidence for public policy.[1]

I am indebted to Paul Evans for diligent research assistance and to Isaac Ehrlich for helpful comments. The support of the Walgreen Foundation for the Study of American Institutions is gratefully acknowledged.

[1] The research on which this study is based is discussed here in nontechnical terms. The interested reader can find still more details in Sam Peltzman, "The Effect of Safety Regulation," *Journal of Political Economy,* vol. 83, no. 4 (July/August 1975), pp. 677-725.

I. THE PROMISE OF SAFETY REGULATION

Specialists in highway safety have produced extensive literature on the effects of highway safety regulation—or, rather, on its expected effects. This is a distinction of some importance, but these expected effects at least provide a starting point for the subsequent analysis, and therefore are worth summarizing here.

The vehicle safety act of 1966 created a regulatory system that is still far from complete. The agency created by the act, the National Highway and Traffic Safety Administration (NHTSA), has let hardly a year pass since 1966 without adding to the safety standards to which new cars sold in the United States must conform. However, the first set of standards, which became legally effective in 1968, is still the most important for lifesaving potential. These standards, which are the focus of this study, required that the following important safety devices be installed on each new car:

(1) seatbelts for all occupants,

(2) energy-absorbing steering column,

(3) windshield designed to resist penetration by an occupant's head and neck,

(4) dual braking system (in which loss of hydraulic pressure at one point still leaves two brakes operative),

(5) padded instrument panel.

In part, these 1968 standards represented only a codification of political demands to which automobile manufacturers were already responding. As the hearings that led to the 1966 act went on, the auto makers thought it appropriate to begin installing some of the devices that would be made mandatory in 1968, even though their previous acceptance in the marketplace had been at best limited.[1] The earliest of these anticipatory moves occurred in 1964, when front lap seatbelts became standard equipment on all new cars even though their previous sales as an option had been small. In 1967, most manufacturers made energy-absorbing steering columns and penetration-resistant windshields standard equip-

---

[1] In 1964, the first year in which seatbelts were standard equipment, the National Safety Council reported that 30 percent of all cars on the road had seatbelts installed. See *Accident Facts* (Chicago: NSC, 1965), p. 53. This implies that a little more than 20 percent of the pre-1964 cars then on the road had seatbelts installed either as an option or after purchase.

ment even though these had chalked up virtually no sales as options. These events appear, then, to be the result more of political pressure than of consumer demand. The response of auto makers may have stemmed simply from their belief that prompt action might prevent harsher legislation. In any event, the usual considerations of marketing strategy had little to do with the sudden proliferation of safety devices before 1968.

Whatever the reason for the installation of safety devices before they were legally required, the technical literature may still provide some idea of the livesaving potential of these devices in some more recent year. While the literature is varied, it commonly focuses on the differences between the experience of accident victims who used a safety device and those who did not. From this comparison, an estimate is typically made of the reduced risk of death or injury to users of the device, adjusted (if the researcher is careful and has the data) for the effects of other devices. For example, in accidents in cars with both padded dashboards and seatbelts, the padded dashboards may provide additional protection only for those drivers who did not use belts. To get from this literature a useful estimate of how many lives these devices might actually be saving requires taking account of the drivers who still fail to use some devices (seatbelts, say) or who own older cars that do not have them. In Table 1, I have used the 1972 rates of device installation and usage to estimate the lifesaving effects of the various safety devices. (The details of these estimates may be found in Appendix A.) The main message of the table is clear; even with incomplete installation and incomplete usage of these safety devices, somewhere between 10 and 25 percent fewer vehicle occupants died in 1972 than one otherwise would have expected. For total deaths—vehicle occupants and pedestrians—this development would represent a reduction of 7.5 to 20 percent. The "consensus" of the estimates is closer to the upper ends of these ranges.

These estimates reflect widespread agreement among those who do research on safety that seatbelts and energy-absorbing steering columns are singularly effective safety devices. For example, in their 1968 study, Donald Huelke and Paul Gikas found that impact from the steering column and ejection from the vehicle alone account for over 40 percent of all fatalities.[2] Their

---

[2] Donald Huelke and Paul Gikas, "Causes of Deaths in Automobile Accidents," *Journal of the American Medical Association* (25 March 1968), pp. 1100-1107.

Table 1

EXPECTED REDUCTION IN OCCUPANT DEATH RATE
DUE TO SELECTED SAFETY DEVICES,
1972 DEVICE INSTALLATION AND USAGE RATES

Device	Source of Estimate	Expected Reduction of Death Rate (percent)
Lap seatbelts	National Safety Council, 1967 et seq.	7-8.5
	Huelke and Gikas, 1968	13
	Levine and Campbell, 1971	16
	Kihlberg, 1969	15
	Joksch and Wuerdeman, 1972	13
	National Highway Traffic Safety Administration, 1968	13.5
	Office of Science & Technology, 1972 [a]	14
Energy-absorbing steering column	Lave and Weber, 1970	4
	Joksch and Wuerdeman, 1972	5
	National Highway Traffic Safety Administration, 1968 [b]	5.5
	Levine and Campbell, 1971	6.5
Shoulder belt	Bohlin, 1967	1
	Joksch and Wuerdeman, 1972	0.25
	Huelke and Gikas, 1968	0.25
	Office of Science & Technology, 1972 [a]	0.25
High-penetration-resistant windshield	National Highway Traffic Safety Administration, 1968	0
	Joksch and Wuerdeman, 1972	2.5
Padded instrument panel	Lave and Weber, 1970	0
Dual braking system	Lave and Weber, 1970	0.5

[a] From Cornell Aeronautical Laboratory data.

[b] From data in Statement by A. Nahum and A. Siegel, University of California, Los Angeles, before U.S. Senate Commerce Committee, 25 April 1968.

Source: The full citation of sources and the derivation of estimates are given in Appendix A. Estimates are rounded to nearest 0.5 percent for lap seatbelts and collapsible steering column; to nearest 0.25 percent for other devices.

research and related research by Lester Lave and Warren Weber [3] suggest that about 70 percent of these deaths could be prevented if seatbelts and energy-absorbing steering columns were univer- sally used. Indeed, the safety literature implies strongly that only

[3] Lester Lave and Warren Weber, "A Benefit-Cost Analysis of Auto Safety Features," *Applied Economics,* vol. 2 (1970), pp. 265-275.

public lethargy in using lap and shoulder belts stands in the way of a tripling or quadrupling of the lives saved.[4]

It would be presumptuous and superfluous to question the medical and engineering expertise underlying the studies summarized in Table 1. But they do have limitations for the specific purpose of determining the effects of safety devices on the highway death toll. If the medical-engineering data are naïvely interpreted, they suggest that upward of 10,000 lives are now saved each year by the Vehicle Safety Act of 1966. This estimate, however, would be exaggerated for at least two reasons: (1) it ignores the adaptations that people would have made in the absence of the act, and (2) it ignores the adaptations that they may have made precisely because of the act.

These adaptations would be spurred by the same sort of rational choices that underlie behavior in, say, the supermarket. Driving and shopping both yield rewards that are purchased at a cost; in the case of driving the cost includes risk of accident and death. The ingredients of this cost are themselves matters of choice. To spend time driving more slowly can reduce the risk of accident and death, but the time spent costs money. If driver behavior is determined by the weighing of rewards and costs, a change in driver behavior brought about by a regulatory change in the structure of rewards and costs should not be surprising.

These elementary ideas have important general implications for the evaluation of safety regulation. For instance, measuring the effect of regulation without asking what driver behavior would have been in its absence would yield misleading answers. Perhaps the lack of accident protection would have induced drivers to drive more carefully. In the absence of the requirement for safety devices, it may be asked whether drivers would have bought them anyway, or whether they would have bought a different car, or whether they would have supported the appeals of a politician for safer highways. The estimates of effectiveness that are given in Table 1 ignore driver adaptations. They tell what might happen if regulation were introduced and no other change occurred. This information will be meaningful only if the changes in fact induced by regulation are trivial. Whether they are trivial is an important empirical question; it cannot be assumed away.

---

[4] The possibility that seatbelts might themselves be lethal sometimes is recognized but dismissed as empirically trivial. See Huelke and Gikas, "Causes of Deaths."

Even a cursory glance at accident data before the 1966 act reveals one of the problems in ignoring driver choices. In most years driving was safer (per mile or vehicle) than it had been the year before. This situation held even as car speeds and alcohol consumption rose, and it would be inexplicable if drivers operated the same cars in the same way on the same kinds of roads year after year. Quite clearly, driving practices, types of cars purchased, and road design were responding, however gradually and unspectacularly, to such factors affecting the cost of safety, broadly defined, as increasing wealth and technological change.[5] It must be asked why these factors should have ceased to have effects on driving had the safety act of 1966 not been passed. Probably, in fact, they would not. The ensuing regulation could well have altered these effects.

At one extreme, the private market may have been ready to "buy" precisely the devices required by law, in which case the regulations had no role other than to confirm market judgments. In light of the poor market performance of these devices before regulation, regulation probably did not play so completely passive a role. Even so, there remains the possibility that the regulation may have been one more of form than of substance and that the safety improvements resulting from the 1968 standards displaced other kinds that would have been produced by market forces. Again, such a question has to be answered empirically: did safety regulation add to, or substitute for, the market forces producing more safety over time, and in either case by how much? The risk in ignoring substitution—as most estimates of the effects of safety regulation do—ought to be obvious. If, in the absence of regulation, drivers voluntarily pay for 10 percent more safety (however measured), and regulation then comes along and forces them to buy this 10 percent, some or all of the voluntary expenditure is likely to be displaced. The net contribution of the regulation to safety will then be under 10 percent.

Another kind of interaction between regulation and private choice can best be understood by supposing that the regulation is effective, in the sense that it forces the purchase of, say, 20 percent more safety when only 10 percent more would otherwise be bought. Here it is necessary to define "purchasing safety" more precisely. The sort of regulation embodied in the 1968 standards

---

[5] Other such factors include not only costs of safety devices or vehicle design, but highway design, medical care, driver education, traffic-law enforcement, and so on.

6

cannot require the purchase of more safety, but only of the devices that can reduce the costs of an accident to life and limb.[6] The distinction is important if the decision to run the risk of an accident is not an immutable outcome of pathological behavior. To return to a previous point, that decision should be conditioned by the rewards and costs of the risk. One result of (effective) safety regulation is to reduce the costs of this risk, and this reduction should induce greater willingness on the part of drivers to run the risk. It is not the risk itself that a driver seeks, but its derivative benefits: getting from one place to another more quickly, permitting a young driver to use the family car, and so on. If those benefits can be purchased at a lower prospective cost—because of a decline in the risk of accident undertaken to produce a given benefit or because of a decline in the cost of the accident associated with a given risk—the amount of benefits sought by drivers may be expected to increase. Most of us are probably familiar with the first response—to reduced risk. We drive faster on expressways than on city streets, and with our more powerful cars, we pass other cars on two-lane roads more frequently. In these circumstances, at least part of the reduction in risk is offset by an increase in accident exposure. There is no reason to expect any markedly different response to required safety devices, even though here it is not risk but rather the costs of accident that are reduced. The logic of choice suggests that drivers would respond to lower cost by incurring greater risk. But logic by itself does not permit an assessment of the net effects on the actual highway death toll. That is, one cannot rule out the possibility that a 20 percent reduction in the cost per accident will lead to a 20 percent—or, for that matter, a 30 percent—increase in the number of accidents. Here, too, the relevant question is an empirical one, but the theory does imply that the effects of safety regulation are likely to be exaggerated if one focuses only on their implications for the cost per accident.

So far, I have raised two distinct empirical points: (1) regulation may have been partly or completely ineffective in that it may have substituted for actions drivers would have taken anyway,

---

[6] While most of the important devices required by the 1966 act are designed to protect occupants after a crash has occurred, accident prevention has not been completely ignored. The most notable example, perhaps, is the requirement for a dual braking system. There are, in addition, about twenty standards in the so-called "100 Series" (accident prevention) of vehicle safety standards that seek to improve lighting and visibility, tire performance, and the like.

and (2) regulation may have had the desired effects, but they may have been offset by additional risk-taking by drivers. How might one distinguish which, if either, of these is the case? The distinction clearly cannot be made by an examination of highway deaths in the aggregate, inasmuch as either point would be consistent with the observed death toll. The distinction would show up in other dimensions of highway accidents—specifically, in the total number of accidents and in the distribution of deaths among vehicle occupants and pedestrians.

Suppose regulation merely substitutes for market forces. In this case, not only would the number of deaths and injuries be the same as would have occurred without regulation, but so would the distribution of deaths and injuries and the number of accidents. But the outcome would be different if regulation effectively lowered the cost of an accident. First, if the lowered cost were offset, it would be through an increase in the number of accidents. Second, while they reduce the cost of an accident for vehicle occupants, safety devices do not reduce the cost for pedestrians. Thus, if the number of accidents should rise, a larger share of the burden of injury and death would be borne by pedestrians. In the next section, I shall try to sort out these empirical issues by an analysis of accidents and of the distribution of deaths and injuries among drivers and pedestrians, as well as of the total death rate.

II. EMPIRICAL EVIDENCE ON THE EFFECTS OF SAFETY REGULATION

The discussion above makes clear that one cannot evaluate the effects of safety regulation without some notion of what would have happened in its absence. But this notion is hard to obtain and never exact, because one cannot observe the same driver in two situations identical in every respect except for the presence or absence of safety regulation. Even so, unless the two are to remain hopelessly confounded, one must make an attempt to disentangle the effect of regulation from the effect of other factors.

To do so, I will first investigate the forces underlying accident rates in the period before federal safety regulation was instituted. Here I will seek answers to such questions as these: How much did vehicle speed, alcohol consumption, and the number of young drivers contribute to death rates? How did changes in drivers' incomes and in the money costs of accidents (car repairs and medical costs) affect the kind of accident risks the drivers ran? Quantitative answers to these questions for the period before regulation can help predict the most likely course of events had regulation not intervened. These estimates may then be compared with actual recent experience. If regulation has attained its goal, the actual death rate should be below the rate likely without regulation.

Influences Operating on Safety, 1947–1965. To carry out the procedure described, I will analyze national death and accident rates in each year from 1947 through 1972. Safety regulation could have had no measurable impact on death rates until the last part of this period, so that the main interest in the earlier years centers on learning what underlies death rates in a world without regulation. For this purpose, I will make use of annual data on accident costs, incomes, driving speeds, driver ages, and alcohol consumption for 1947 through 1965 (the last year that may reasonably be treated as essentially unaffected by regulation). The object is to establish the extent to which each factor contributed to each year's death rate. These factors are not the sole contributors to highway deaths, but as a group their contribution has been substantial. Moreover, statistical theory, if not the demands of intelligibility, makes it inadvisable to consider any more factors.[1]

Three of these factors—alcohol, age, and speed—have long been mentioned as leading contributors to highway fatalities. Frequent reports implicate alcohol in half of fatal accidents [2] and show that young drivers are disproportionately involved. Highway deaths per capita are consistently around 50 percent higher for those aged fifteen to twenty-four than for the rest of the population, and among drivers involved in fatal accidents the disparity is wider yet. The role of speed is somewhat more

---

[1] Some of the additional factors that I tried to take account of, but that failed to improve upon the statistical analysis of death rates reported here, are worth noting. These included the average age of cars, the ratio of new cars to all cars (because it has been suggested that while drivers familiarize themselves with their new cars, accident risk may increase), traffic density, expenditures on traffic-law enforcement by state highway patrols, expenditures on roads, the ratio of imports to total cars (because there is evidence that small cars are more lethal than large cars if an accident occurs), education of the population, and the availability of hospital care (which might reduce deaths if injury occurs).

[2] National Safety Council, *Accident Facts,* 1972, p. 52.

ambiguous. A large proportion of fatal accidents occur at high speeds, but so does a large proportion of all driving.[3] Nevertheless, the belief that "speed kills" is so deeply ingrained into legal institutions that a more rigorous statistical analysis of its effects is clearly warranted.

The roles played by income and accident costs are less familiar. By accident costs I mean the money outlay that a driver can expect to incur if he is involved in an accident. Much of this outlay is covered by insurance, and if insurance companies never used experience rating (which adjusts a driver's premiums according to his accident record), the outlay would be negligible for insured drivers. But insurers do in general engage in experience rating, so that a driver can expect to pay back some of the costs created in an accident through higher future premiums. My assumption here is that this expectation will deter drivers from taking accident risks. More precisely, the greater the expected premium increase the less willing drivers will be to take risks now.

Changes in income can have diverse—even offsetting—effects on the risks drivers take. These changes will work partly through forces I have already mentioned; for example, both alcohol consumption and the number of fast cars owned increase with income. But other forces spur more risk-taking as income rises. When wages increase or the opportunity for gainful work-time activity expands, drivers will have an added incentive to spend less time commuting. They will thus commute at higher speeds (though these may be imperfectly reflected in the measures that are directly available, which relate to vehicles on rural roads at off-peak hours), and with more risk-taking generally—greater willingness to take short cuts, pass other cars, and so on. However, rising incomes should also produce offsetting effects. They should enable drivers to afford safer cars and should also (more indirectly) enlarge the tax base for expenditures on public safety, including road improvements. Higher wages also make the consequences of an accident that impairs earning capacity more serious. Only an empirical analysis can establish the net effect of these conflicting forces.

Such an analysis faces two problems: separating the effects of the various factors and separating long-run from short-run

---

[3] For example, the National Safety Council (in 1972) reported that 30 percent of rural fatal accidents occurred at speeds in excess of 60 miles per hour. However, according to Federal Highway Administration data, 50 percent of traffic on main rural roads moved at speeds over 60 miles per hour in the same year.

effects. To illustrate the first problem, even if alcohol is involved in many fatal accidents, some drinking drivers may also be young or may have been driving at high speeds. Some fatal accidents that involve alcohol might therefore have occurred anyway. The point is the *net* effect of alcohol—how many *more* deaths would occur from heavier alcohol consumption if all other circumstances remained the same. Fortunately, this sort of problem is amenable to conventional statistical techniques, which have yielded the data discussed subsequently. (The technical detail is relegated to Appendix B.)

The role of income exemplifies the need for distinguishing short-run from long-run effects. New cars are purchased infrequently, so a driver with enhanced work opportunities may well react first by driving his present car faster and then by buying a car that makes high-speed driving safer. The general economic principle at work here is the greater costliness of making large adjustments all at once rather than gradually, and its application is not limited to the effects of income. The immediate effects of additional young drivers on the road or of increased alcohol consumption can be countered by more vigilant law enforcement or better public education, but usually some time elapses between the perception of the desirability of these measures and their implementation.

A glance at the relevant data shows the importance of distinguishing short-run from long-run adjustments. Virtually everything that might contribute to highway deaths—alcohol consumption, traffic speeds, the proportion of drivers under twenty-five, incomes—has increased over time. Yet the highway death rate has tended to fall. A naïve inference might be that rich young people who speed after a few drinks actually are safer drivers. The more sensible inference would be that the cumulative effects of long-run adjustments by drivers and public authorities to the dangers of speed and alcohol have tended generally to outweigh the short-run effects of the increases in these factors. It would then follow that, with the same long-run adjustments and no increases in speed and alcohol consumption, the long-term downtrend of the death rate ought to have been even more pronounced. In fact, this sort of interpretation is not only intuitively appealing, but also consistent with the data, as is discussed more fully below. Unfortunately, it is possible only partially to disentangle long-run from short-run adjustments. The available data and statistical techniques permit an estimate of only the total impact of all long-run adjustments in a typical year's death rate; the long-run adjustment to higher income cannot be separated from that to heavier drinking. Only the sum of such adjustments can be measured. Nor can years of atypically weak or atypically powerful long-run adjustments be identified; only the average adjustment is available.

The main findings of the statistical investigation into the factors underlying the highway death rate in the period before regulation of safety became effective are summarized in Table 2. (More detailed description and the sources of the underlying data can be found in Appendix B.) The death rate analyzed, measured per vehicle mile, is adjusted for changes in the urban-rural composition of driving (rural driving is more lethal than urban driving) and for changes in the share of traffic on limited-access highways

Table 2

FACTORS UNDERLYING THE HIGHWAY DEATH RATE, 1947–1965

A 1 percent increase in:	(1) Led, on average, to a short-run change in the death rate of:	(2) The average annual change of the variable was:	(3) = (1) × (2) The average annual short-run contribution of the variable to the death rate was to increase it by:
1. Alcohol consumption (per adult)	0.4%	1.3%	0.5%
2. Vehicle speed (off-peak hours, rural roads)	1.8	1.2	2.1
3. Ratio of 15-24 year-olds to older population	0.8	0.7	0.6
4. Income (earned, per working-age adult)	0.9	2.1	1.9
5. Accident cost	− 0.2	− 1.2	0.2
6. Total short-run contribution of all variables per year (sum of 1 through 5, column 3)			5.3%
7. Average annual effect of all long-run adjustments			− 7.4
8. Average annual change in the death rate (6 + 7)			− 1.9%

Notes: The death rate is adjusted for changes in rural-urban and interstate-noninterstate highway composition of driving (see text), and the rate is per vehicle mile. Income and accident costs are deflated by general price index. Discrepancies between column (3) and column (1) × (2) are due to rounding. See text and Appendix B for detail and elaboration.

(whose death rate is considerably lower than that on conventional roads).

The data in Table 2 become more meaningful in focusing on a specific factor—for example, speed. In the postwar period, if speed increased by 1 percent, the immediate result was, on average, a 1.8 percent increase in the death rate (column 1, line 2). In fact, in a typical year vehicle speeds increased more than 1 percent—about 1.2 percent (column 2, line 2), so that the typical impact of faster driving speeds in any year was to push the death rate up by over 2 percent (column 3, line 2). Indeed, column 3 shows that vehicle speed was the single most important short-run cause of the higher death rates in the postwar period.

The short-run effects of rising incomes were next in importance—that is, the net immediate impact of an economic expansion was to raise death rates. Interestingly, these two factors vastly overshadow alcohol consumption and driver age over the whole period from 1947 to 1965. At least for age, this was true only because important effects worked in different directions at various times within this period.

The sum of all short-run forces is given on line 6 of Table 2. Obviously, since such factors as income and vehicle speed have generally increased, this sum also shows an increase—which means that had there been no response to the greater vehicle speeds, alcohol consumption, and so on, the trend of the death rate would have been up (by over 5 percent per year), not down. But these dangerous forces were in fact more than offset by the long-run responses to their increase on the part of drivers and others. These responses pulled the death rate down about 7 percent annually (line 7), so that the net death rate declined 2 percent annually on the average.

Figure 1 provides some indication of the way in which the postwar death-rate experience mirrors these short- and long-run forces. The solid line shows the course of the death rate from 1947 to 1965, and the dashed line depicts the death rate that one could have estimated knowing the weights in column (1) of Table 2 and the year-by-year changes in each of the five contributing factors. The two lines are never more than 2 percent apart, suggesting that these five factors explain all but the last mystery of the death rate. In particular, these factors and the responses made to them were pushing the death rate downward rapidly from 1947 to 1954, further downward but less rapidly to 1961, and upward from 1961 to 1965.

Figure 1

HIGHWAY DEATH RATE, 1947–1965

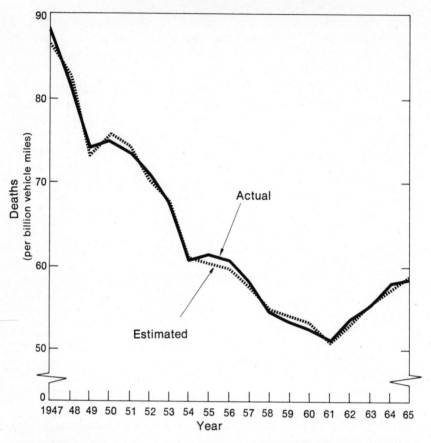

Behind this pattern, did any of these five factors have a decisive role first in slowing and then in reversing the decline in the death rate? If one culprit is to be singled out, it would have to be demographic change. The decline in the birth rate that began before the Great Depression ended in the mid-1930s and the subsequent rise culminated in the postwar "baby boom." These demographic developments are reflected, with an appropriate lag, in shifts in the proportions of young to old drivers, which go far toward explaining what happened to highway deaths. In Figure 2, the whole period from 1947 to 1965 is broken down into three subperiods. For each, the average annual percentage change in the death rate is shown by the unshaded bar. The shaded bar shows the change that (given the information in

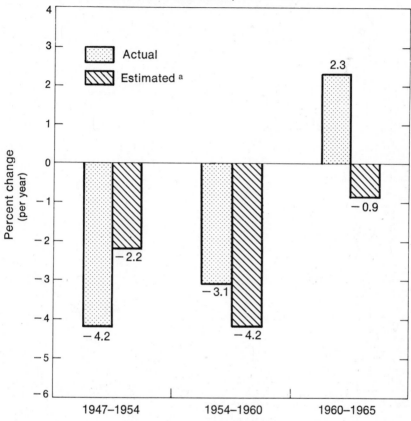

Figure 2

AVERAGE ANNUAL CHANGES IN DEATH RATE,
THREE SUBPERIODS, 1947–1965

□ Actual

▨ Estimated [a]

a If ratio of 15-24 year olds to rest of population had not changed.

Table 2) could have been expected had the age composition of the population remained stable. If the birth rate had not begun to increase in the 1930s, there would have been an accelerated, rather than retarded, decline in the death rate in the late 1950s. Without a postwar baby boom, a moderate decline, rather than an increase, would have occurred in the death rate after 1960.

The early 1960s turn out to have produced an unusually hostile environment for highway safety. Not only were the demographic forces exceedingly unfavorable, but, as the figure shows, the other factors provided little offset. In particular, this period was marked by recovery from a recession (with con-

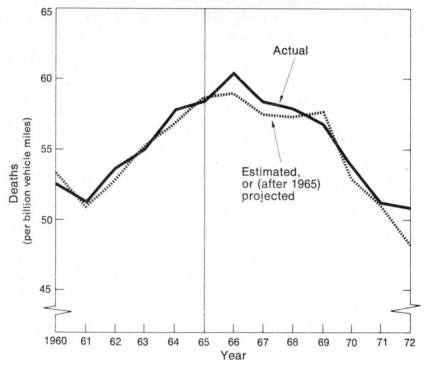

Figure 3

HIGHWAY DEATH RATE, 1960–1972

comitant increased growth in alcohol consumption) and a growing popularity of cars with high horsepower. This experience of the early 1960s may help explain why Congress felt a need to do something about highway safety.

The Effect of Safety Regulation, 1966–1972. What was actually accomplished by the 1966 safety act? The basic facts about the death rate are clear. The rise in the death rate halted after 1965 and in fact was reversed. But how much credit goes to safety regulation and how much to the less dangerous environment of the late 1960s? The answer is uncertain, but clearly the safety act was not solely responsible. Figure 3 repeats part of Figure 1 and shows in addition the most likely course of the death rate (shown by the dashed line) in light of the experience before regulation (summarized in Table 2), and in light of the behavior of the five contributing factors after 1965.

16

Since the weights attached to each of the five factors (from column 1, Table 2) are derived entirely from experience before safety regulation took hold, the projections indicate the most likely death rate assuming no safety regulation and no change in the factors contributing to highway deaths. The death rates without regulation turn out to be not much different from those experienced with regulation. The projected and actual rates stay within 2 percent of each other except for 1972, when the actual rate is 4 percent higher. If safety regulation had contributed to a reduction in highway deaths, over and above the reduction past experience would have suggested, actual death rates should be lower than the projections by steadily widening amounts. If Table 1 is to be believed, this gap ought to have been something like 20 percent by 1972. But nothing like this occurred; indeed, with regulation, even more deaths occurred in 1972 than would have been expected without regulation. The most tenable conclusion is that evidence for a measurable effect of safety regulation on highway deaths is lacking. The 1966 peak and the subsequent decline in the death rate can be explained entirely by non-regulatory forces, the most important of which was demographic. The peaking of the birth rate around 1950 led to slower growth of the population of driving age under twenty-five by the late 1960s. Moreover, the rise in income and vehicle speeds slowed, and rising medical and car-repair costs added a deterrent to risk-taking.

Did safety regulation have any effects at all? Did it fail to reduce highway deaths because it substituted required expenditures on safety for those that drivers might otherwise have made? Or did drivers react to the required devices by taking more risk of accident? One way to shed light on these questions is to look at the distribution of deaths and injuries among drivers and pedestrians. If drivers took more risks because of the added protection afforded by safety devices, the outcome would be a higher death rate for pedestrians (unless, of course, pedestrians took correspondingly greater precautions against less careful drivers).

Some evidence indeed appears to suggest that pedestrians have fared worse than drivers since regulation was imposed. This evidence is summarized in Table 3, which shows the actual and projected death and injury rates for 1972 separately for pedestrians and motor-vehicle occupants. The projected rates are derived using the same sort of technique underlying Figure 3. (The interested reader can find the weights analogous to those in

Table 3
DEATH AND INJURY RATES, 1972

Deaths or Injuries	1972 Rate (per billion vehicle miles)		Percentage by Which Actual Exceeds Projected $(3) = \dfrac{(1) - (2)}{(2)}$
	Actual (1)	Projected (2)	
Deaths:			
(1) Vehicle occupants	38.6	41.4	−7.3
(2) Pedestrians	12.0	8.4	42.9
(3) Total	50.6	48.3	4.7
Injuries:			
(4) Vehicle occupants	1,740	1,630	6.8
(5) Pedestrians	170	130	30.8
(6) Total	1,910	1,730	10.4

Notes: Rates are adjusted for change in urban-rural driving mix and in proportion to traffic on limited-access highways. See text and Appendix B.

The projected totals (lines 3 and 6, column 2) are estimated separately from the components, and because of this they differ slightly from the total of the projected components.

Pedestrians include bicyclists and motorcyclists.

Table 2 for total deaths in Appendix B.[4]) Note first that safety devices seem to have some lifesaving effect for vehicle occupants; they suffered about 7 percent fewer deaths than could have been expected otherwise (line 1). This is only a fraction of the lifesaving potential of these devices, and the statistical significance of the estimate is questionable. In any case, any saving of occupants' lives is offset by the substantial excess of pedestrian deaths over expectations, assuming no safety regulation. Only a small part of this excess can be explained by the recent unusual increase in the number of bicycle and motorcycle riders, who are included with pedestrians.[5] The last three lines of Table 3 reveal a similar pattern for injuries, except that here even drivers do not appear to be spared injuries by safety devices. Again, pedestrians have much worse experience than vehicle occupants do.

[4] More complete data, for the years 1965-1972, are in Peltzman, "Effect of Safety Regulation."

[5] See note 19, Appendix B.

Pushing the analysis one stage further, if pedestrians now incur more deaths and injuries because drivers are less careful, the total number of accidents not involving death or injury should also have increased above what could have been expected without safety regulation. In fact, they seem to have done so. The property-damage accident rate that could have been projected for 1972 in the absence of safety regulation was about 11,000 per billion vehicle miles. The actual rate for 1972 was roughly 15,000, or over 30 percent greater.[6] This figure translates into nearly 4 million additional accidents.

Finally, the highway-safety literature leads one to expect a 20 or 25 percent reduction in the risk of death *per accident*, and in fact a reduction quite close to that seems to have been realized. But the findings here indicate that these devices have stimulated an increase in the *number* of accidents—of 25 percent or more. The net effect on the death rate has been insignificant.

III. FURTHER EVIDENCE ON EFFECTS OF SAFETY REGULATION

These findings on the net results of the enforced installation of safety devices must provoke some skepticism, not because they are inconsistent with economic theory but because of the sheer magnitude of the forces offsetting the direct effects of safety devices. Therefore, I examined other kinds of data to see if they might offer any corroboration for the findings. One possibility was that some general weakening in the forces that would tend to decrease the death rate coincided with, but was offset by, safety regulation.

A possibility of this kind can never be ruled out, and though its significance may not be susceptible to direct measurement, it can be measured indirectly. For example, if the forces limiting the death rate had weakened generally, the death rate in an area in which no cars were equipped with safety devices should have been higher in 1972 than in 1965. Or, provided that safety devices really do reduce deaths, the death rate should have been greater in that area than in a similar area where most cars were equipped with the devices. No such neat comparison is available in the real world, because in every area in the United States, and indeed in most other industrialized countries, substantial numbers of cars have been equipped with safety devices, and if they have

---

[6] See Peltzman, "Effect of Safety Regulation," for details of the calculation.

not it is only because they are unusually old, and car age itself may affect death rates. Moreover, the superficial similarities of areas may conceal quite different changes between 1965 and the date of comparison in important factors underlying the death rate.

Death Rates and Prevalence of Safety Devices. In light of these problems, I have attempted to compare the death-rate experience of the different states since 1965, after adjustment for other factors (including the pure effect of car age). The question was whether the experience was more favorable where cars equipped with safety devices were introduced relatively rapidly. I will refer the reader elsewhere for the details of the comparison,[1] but the basic result will show up in a comparison less refined than the one made there. In Table 4 the forty-eight conterminous states are presented in four groups, defined by the 1971 proportions of their cars equipped with the federally required devices. By 1971 about three-quarters of all cars on the road had at least some of these devices, but the ratio was less than two-thirds in some states and close to nine-tenths in others. If these devices have had an effect, after regulation the death rates should have been rising least in the states where newer cars were more prevalent (Group I in Table 4). In fact, the table reveals a slightly steeper rise (or lesser fall) in death rates in those states. This finding should not be given great weight, however. The most that can be said is that the proportion of its cars equipped with safety devices has virtually no relation to a state's highway death rate, just as the previous evidence suggested. On the other hand, contrary to the previous evidence, the share of deaths borne by pedestrians in a state was found to be unrelated to the proportion of cars equipped with safety devices (though the data were fragmentary).[2]

This last finding casts some doubt on the notion that safety regulation is ineffective because it leads to more risky driving. Perhaps something other than safety regulation has been behind the unexpectedly high accident rates of recent years. For example, which drivers are having the accidents? Are drivers of cars equipped with safety devices having a disproportionate share of the accidents?

Unfortunately, no readily available U.S. data can help answer this question. However, for a few of the provinces, the Canadian

---

[1] Peltzman, "Effect of Safety Regulation."

[2] See ibid. for the relevant data.

Table 4

PERCENTAGE CHANGE IN HIGHWAY DEATH RATES
OF STATES RANKED BY AGE OF CAR STOCK,
BY SELECTED VARIABLES, 1963–64 TO 1971–72

	Percentage Change in Deaths [b]			
States [a]	Per capita	Per licensed driver	Per registered vehicle	Per gallon of highway fuel consumed
Group I	16.6	6.8	− 8.9	− 22.6
Group II	14.3	0.4	− 10.5	− 24.0
Group III	9.8	− 8.0	− 14.8	− 30.6
Group IV	14.8	1.7	− 10.7	− 24.7

[a] Forty-eight states divided into four equal groups according to the share in total 1971 registrations of autos built in 1964 and later years. Group I has the highest share, group IV the lowest.

[b] Percentage changes are computed from aggregate data for each group of twelve states. Reliable state data on vehicle miles are unavailable for 1963-1964.

Sources: Deaths—National Safety Council, *Accident Facts,* various years; licensed drivers' fuel consumption—Federal Highway Administration, *Highway Statistics* (Washington, D.C.: U.S. Government Printing Office, various years); vehicle registrations—R. L. Polk and Co., *Passenger Cars: Registration Counts by Make and Year of Model* (Detroit: R. L. Polk and Co., various years).

government has published data on accidents classified by the model year of the car involved. Because Canada has adopted precisely the same set of safety regulations as the United States did, the Canadian data bear directly on the U.S. relationship of regulation to accident risk.

A simple comparison of the accident records of cars equipped with safety devices and of older cars would be misleading, because car age itself affects the frequency with which accidents are reported and perhaps actual frequency as well.[3] One can, however, compare accident frequencies for cars of the same age in the years before and after regulation became effective, as in Table 5. The age groups are chosen to include 1964 and later model years in the period after regulation. The percentage of all accidents involving these post-1963 models is then compared to that involving cars in the same age class for the years from 1959 to 1963. In every year since 1964 cars subject to regulation have

[3] There are legal minimums on the property damage requiring a report, so older cars report fewer accidents.

Table 5

PERCENTAGE OF ALL REPORTED ACCIDENTS
INVOLVING CARS IN VARIOUS AGE GROUPS,
BEFORE AND AFTER 1964 (CANADA)

Age of Cars [a]	After 1964: Yearly Accident Rates for Cars Mfd. after 1963		Before 1964: Accident Rates for Cars of Comparable Ages (Avg., 1959–63)
	Year	Rates	
1 year	1964	12.7%	10.4%
2 years	1965	27.9	23.7
3 years	1966	39.3	35.2
4 years	1967	50.7	45.9
5 years	1968	61.2	55.4
6 years	1969	70.7	64.0
7 years	1970	76.1	72.5
8 years	1971	83.5	79.6
9 years	1972	89.0	85.4

[a] Each group includes all cars up to the given age.
Source: Accident data from Statistics Canada, *Motor Vehicle Traffic Accidents* (Ottawa, various years).

accounted for a larger share of accidents than the same age class did before regulation. This consistency is the significant point, not the magnitude of the differences between the before- and after-regulation frequencies. For one thing, as the age range becomes more inclusive and thus the groups being compared grow larger, the differences narrow automatically; that is, once one establishes an age group that includes the oldest cars on the road, that group must account for 100 percent of all the accidents. In addition, differences in accident frequency can be affected by differences in the share of the car stock accounted for by any age group. Appendix B reports an attempt to infer from the data used in Table 4 the average accident frequency of the typical post-1964 car after taking account of both this factor and car age. It turns out that, on average, a post-1964 car has about a 25 percent greater chance of being involved in an accident than a car of the same age did before 1964. This is roughly consistent with the data on U.S. accidents presented earlier.

Similar evidence comes from data on accidents in North Carolina. Levine and Campbell used a sample of North Carolina accidents occurring in 1966 and 1968 to cars built in 1964 and after, classified by presence or absence of an energy-absorbing steering column (and implicitly the other devices introduced simultaneously; thus all cars in the sample have seatbelts).[4] Data on car registration in North Carolina show that no more than 27 percent of all cars eligible for the sample in the two years were equipped with the energy-absorbing column,[5] but such cars accounted for 34 percent of all accidents in the sample. This implies that cars with the safety devices are 40 percent more likely to have accidents than cars without them.

Factors in Driver Risk-Taking. If drivers do indeed adjust to safety devices by running more risk of accidents, how do they make this adjustment? The preceding analysis demonstrated that accident risk is related to driving speed, the age of drivers, and alcohol consumption. The next question is whether driving speed, driving by the young, and drunken driving have increased in the aftermath of safety regulation.

Driving speed. To get evidence on driving speed, I followed the procedure used to obtain evidence on death rates. I estimated the underlying determinants of speed before 1965, and used them to estimate speeds after 1965 had there been no safety regulation. This exercise does not suggest that safety regulation served to increase driving speed (at least in rural areas at off-peak hours); the projections were all within 1 or 2 percent of the actual speeds.[6] In making these projections, I did not, however, take account of legal inhibitions on speed. Speed limits have changed little in the last fifteen years, and by the late 1960s actual driving speeds had begun to bump against them. In 1960, only 20 percent of all cars on non-interstate rural roads were exceeding 60 miles per hour, which is roughly the (pre-1974) national average limit. This percentage doubled to 40 by 1965, then increased only 10 percentage points in the next seven years. In part, tighter speed laws may have overcome any tendency for safety devices to stimulate higher driving speeds in rural areas.

---

[4] Donald Levine and B. J. Campbell, "Effectiveness of Lap Seatbelts and the Energy Absorbing System in the Reduction of Injuries," mimeograph (Chapel Hill: University of North Carolina, Highway Safety Research Center, 1971).

[5] R. L. Polk and Company, *Passenger Cars: Registration Counts by Make and Year of Model* (Detroit: R. L. Polk and Co., various years).

[6] See Appendix B for the regression equation from which these projections were made.

23

Driver age. Another channel through which safety regulation might work to increase risk is driver age. Unfortunately, data on driver age in the pre-regulation period are sketchy, but piecing together some available data makes it possible to trace the propensities of different age groups to drive before and after the advent of regulation. Table 6, which shows the ratio of drivers to nondrivers for different age groups in 1958, 1965, and 1972 indicates some loosened restraint on driving by the young in the years after regulation. In the seven years before 1965, the proportion of older people who became drivers increased, while the driving proportion of the young decreased slightly. After 1965 the propensity of older people to drive maintained about the same upward trend. But whatever had previously been inhibiting driving by the young must have lost some of its force, for the

Table 6
RATIO OF DRIVERS TO NONDRIVERS BY AGE, 1958, 1965, AND 1972

Year and Series	Ratio of Drivers to Nondrivers		Percentage Change in Ratio From Earlier Year	
	Under 25 (1)	25 and older (2)	Under 25 (3)	25 and older (4)
1958 NSC	2.88	2.13	—	—
1965 NSC	2.66	2.99	−7.6	40.3
1965 FHA	2.91	3.01	—	—
1972 FHA	3.42	4.16	17.5	38.2

Note: Before 1965, the NSC (National Safety Council, *Accident Facts,* various years) was the sole source of data on the age distribution of drivers. Since 1965, the FHA (Federal Highway Administration) has published similar data (see National Highway Traffic Safety Administration, *A Report on Activities Under the National Traffic and Motor Vehicle Safety Act,* 1973, p. A23). The data in column 1 are adjusted to account for the effects of lower driver participation of those under twenty and shifts in the age composition of those under twenty-five. Specifically, the ratio of drivers to population (p) is calculated separately for the age cohorts sixteen to nineteen and twenty to twenty-four in each year. These are combined into a weighted average ($\bar{p}$) with fixed weights of 0.478 and 0.522, which are the 1958-1972 average proportions of these subcohorts in the sixteen to twenty-four cohort. The data in column 1 are $\bar{p}/(1 - \bar{p})$. The unadjusted data for column 1 would be 2.90, 2.65, 2.86, and 3.46 reading from top to bottom.
Percentage changes are calculated from data from the same source.

proportion of drivers among the young stopped declining and began to rise. Note that even in the earlier period, the *number* of young drivers increased, because the number of people under twenty-five rose by enough to overcome the decline in the propensity to drive. What the data imply is that the increase in the number of young drivers since 1965 might have been smaller if some influence had not acted to reverse the previous decline in driver participation. Firmer data would be required to support a conclusion that that influence was safety regulation—data, for example, on the specific car models to which young drivers have had increasing access. But the crude data lend weight to the notion that regulation played a role in loosening the restrictions that parents (or the young themselves) placed on youthful driving.

Drunken driving. The data on drunken driving also point toward more risk-taking by drivers after regulation. As Table 7 shows, until 1965 arrests for drunkenness, drunk driving, and all other minor crimes were declining modestly or remaining essen-

Table 7

ARREST RATES FOR DRUNKENNESS, DRUNK DRIVING, AND OTHER NONSERIOUS CRIMES, SELECTED YEARS

	Arrest Rates (per 1,000)			Percentage Change in Arrest Rate from Earlier Year		
Year	Drunk driving (per driver)	Drunkenness (per person 15 and older)	Other nonserious crimes (per person 15 and older)	Drunk driving	Drunkenness	Other nonserious crimes
1953	4.45	23.81	22.20	—	—	—
1959	3.85	21.69	24.59	−13.5	−9.1	10.7
1965	3.53	16.60	23.11	−8.3	−23.4	−6.0
1971	5.75	13.32	29.30	62.9	−19.8	26.8

Note: Data are from U.S. Federal Bureau of Investigation, *Crime in the United States* (Washington, D.C.: U.S. Government Printing Office, various years). Prior to 1960, data are available for urban areas only. Therefore, pre-1960 rates are estimates obtained by multiplying reported arrests by the 1960-1961 ratio of total to urban arrests. Reported arrests were divided by population in the areas covered by the FBI survey (pre-1960 population is estimated in a manner similar to arrests) and multiplied by the national ratios of population to the relevant subgroup.

See *Crime in the United States* for definition of nonserious crimes. Drunkenness and drunk driving are separate subcategories.

tially stable. Since 1965, arrests for drunkenness unrelated to driving have continued to fall, arrests for minor crimes have increased somewhat, but arrests for drunk driving have increased substantially—more than twice as fast as those for other minor crimes.

There is, to be sure, a factor complicating any simple linkage of the increase in arrests for drunk driving to safety regulation. In recent years, many states have adopted "implied consent" laws, which require drunk-driving suspects to take breath-analysis tests on pain of revocation of their driving licenses. This practice makes it easier for the police to obtain evidence of drunk driving, though it also requires greater attention to the suspects' constitutional rights. I am unaware of any data that can distinguish the effects of such laws from the effects of an increase in actual drunkenness. It is worth noting, however, that the annual expansion of alcohol consumption has roughly doubled since 1965, so that the rapid increase in drunk-driving arrests is unlikely to be due entirely to legal changes.

Summary. The evidence, tentative though it must be, is broadly consistent with some increase in driver risk-taking since the advent of safety regulation. Certainly none of the data suggest less risk-taking, and most point to some increase. This observation has an important bearing on the way one interprets the main finding of this study—that safety regulation has failed to reduce the highway death rate. On one interpretation, the failure might mean only that regulation has confirmed market forces leading to a reduction in deaths. But in that case, there should have been no marked departure from previous trends in driver risk-taking. The fact that risk-taking does seem to have increased makes it plausible to assume that regulation has lowered the real cost of an accident by more than market forces would have permitted, but in doing so it has stimulated an offsetting series of driver responses.

However one chooses to interpret them, the findings of this study contrast sharply with the apparent intent of safety regulation. When Congress passed the 1966 safety act, it undoubtedly did not act out of a desire either to encourage more accidents, or merely to confirm market forces. It sought, rather, to reduce death rates, but failed to consider the pitfalls in its naïve acceptance of the promise of safety regulation.

IV. IMPLICATIONS FOR PUBLIC POLICY ON REGULATION OF HIGHWAY SAFETY

This study may offer lessons not only for the regulation of vehicle design, but also for broader aspects of highway safety regulation. Until Congress repealed the requirement, laid down by the National Highway Traffic Safety Administration, for seatbelt ignition interlocks in 1974, it appeared that regulation of vehicle design would expand without restriction. Even now, the air bag is almost certain to become mandatory, and Congress has recently extended its authority over highway safety to encompass local speed limits. Clearly, Congress has yet to question the basic rationale for safety regulation.

Yet some questions may well be in order. One concerns the size of the problem that Congress wishes to address. No one doubts the desirability of reducing death rates, on the highway or elsewhere. But since drivers as well as legislators cherish this aim, it did not require regulation to mobilize forces that have already brought about substantial improvements in highway safety and that promise even more. According to the foregoing analysis, safety regulation has, up to now, failed to improve on this record. I think it can be argued plausibly that, even had the ignition interlock remained on the books, expanded regulation of vehicle design would still be unlikely to improve on nonregulatory forces.

One way to argue this point is to estimate the death rate to be expected in, say, 1980, if the nonregulatory forces were permitted to work alone. To make this estimate, I use the information in Table 2, with the following assumptions:

First, the recent above-average inflation of the costs of medical care and car repair will cease, and thereby remove one limit on accidents.

Second, income, alcohol consumption, and speed will increase at their recent rates (up to 1972). The effects of the rise in gasoline prices and of the national maximum speed limit are ignored here.

Third, the fraction of the driving-age population under twenty-five will remain unchanged, as the Census Bureau currently projects.

Fourth, one-quarter of all traffic will move on limited-access roads, compared with one-fifth today, and the urban-rural driving mix will not change.

On these assumptions, and with only nonregulatory forces at work, the death rate will be 33 per billion vehicle miles by 1980.

In 1971 the National Highway Traffic Safety Administration, in ignorance of the subsequent change in gasoline prices but using the likely course of safety regulation, established as its 1980 target a rate of 36 per billion vehicle miles.[1] The nation ought then to be disappointed if this goal is not achieved. But it can legitimately question the desirability of expanding the regulation of vehicle design in the effort to achieve a goal that can be achieved without it—especially when taking the regulatory route may involve more accidents, to say nothing of the costs of safety devices themselves. Thus, if Congress perceives its problem to be improvement upon nonregulatory forces in reducing highway deaths, regulation of vehicle design as currently constituted promises to be a costly nonsolution to the problem.

How costly might a real solution be? With no ready answer, I can only note that Congress may have already hinted that the cost is too high. Almost certainly, at some level of vehicle design, the death rate could be effectively reduced. In other words, if the probability of the death of an occupant from an accident approaches zero, only pedestrians will be left to bear any consequences from increased driver risk-taking. But congressional repeal of the ignition-interlock requirement suggests some recognition that the costs of the design changes needed for significant reductions in the death rate are greater than the benefits would be. And, if the interlock system appears to have failed a cost-benefit test and was therefore dropped, what recommends maintenance of other extant requirements or the imposition of new ones, such as air bags, for which the cost-benefit calculus is similar?

My skepticism about the efficacy of the regulation of vehicle design calls for attention to the problem of relevant alternatives, on two levels. First, what legal intervention would be likely to reduce death rates at a lower cost than design regulation? Second, how strong is the case for such intervention? The answer to the first question is suggested by the basic analytical framework of this study, which holds that design regulation encourages a trade of more accident risk for a lower cost per accident. Any more effective procedure would have to reduce both the risk and the severity of accident simultaneously. Of the many ways of accomplishing this objective, some of the more obvious suggest the motive behind my second question. Governments could levy

---

[1] U.S. National Highway Traffic Safety Administration, *A Report on Activities Under the National Traffic and Motor Vehicle Safety Act* (Washington, D. C.: U.S. Government Printing Office, 1971).

heavier penalties for involvement in accidents and raise the penalty according to the severity of the accident, but a legislature would be unlikely to tax the estate of a dead victim. Legislatures have also been reluctant to restrict driving to those over twenty-five, or to adopt penalties for drunk driving as severe as those in the Scandinavian countries, even though these steps would very likely reduce the number of accidents and deaths.

One extremely important measure that legislatures have been willing to take deserves some attention—the imposition of legal speed limits. To be sure, the effects of a speed limit can be offset in part by less careful driving at lower speeds. However, unlike the influence of design regulation, an effective speed limit at least pushes against both components of the death rate—limiting both the probability and the severity of accidents rather than stimulating an increase in one of them. As an empirical matter, speed limits do appear to work. States with lower limits have lower death rates,[2] though one may legitimately suggest that speed limits also reflect local driving habits. It would be fully consistent with my basic empirical results to credit the national maximum speed limit of 55 miles per hour with much of the recent decline in fatalities.[3] I must add, however, that this limit may currently be no more restrictive than previous limits, inasmuch as the rise in gasoline prices that initially stimulated it could have been expected to reduce driving speeds by as much as the law did.[4]

Putting these caveats aside, suppose that speed limits are an effective constraint. Are they worthwhile? The question implies that the saving of life is costly, and that at some point the costs may be exorbitant; otherwise, speed limits drastically below 55 would be only the first step. The most important and easily grasped cost of a speed limit is the extra time it exacts to accomplish driving tasks, and the correspondingly smaller amount of time available for work or leisure activities. To put this idea in

---

[2] See Peltzman, "Effect of Safety Regulation," for detailed evidence.

[3] Speed limits are never fully enforced, and some driving is done below the limit. But the empirical relationship between speed limits and actual driving speeds is that a 10 percent reduction in the former tends to reduce the latter by 4 percent. This sort of combination is implicit in the enactment of the 55 mile-per-hour limit, and it would translate into something over a 7 percent expected reduction in the death rate, or about half the 1974 decline in the death rate.

[4] In the year after the OPEC oil embargo, gasoline prices rose about one-quarter more rapidly than the prices of other goods. From the analysis of the effects of gasoline prices on driving speed in Appendix B, such a change could be expected to reduce driving speeds by around 5 percent.

context, imagine a community of 125,000 drivers, each driving 10,000 miles per year at an average of 40 miles per hour. (This community is merely the United States in 1972 scaled down to 1/1,000.) In that year, workers earned about $4.50 per hour, which can serve as a rough measure of the value of an hour spent in driving. Now suppose that a new speed limit results in a 1 percent reduction in average driving speed, so that each of the 125,000 drivers spends two and one-half more hours per year behind the wheel than before. In the aggregate, the drivers lose time worth around $1.4 million. From the empirical results of this study, this sum can be expected to buy the following benefits: 1 death less that year, 31 fewer injuries, and 259 fewer property-damage accidents. What is a plausible estimate of these benefits? The usual procedure in evaluating life and limb is to measure the loss in earning productivity. On this basis, the NHTSA estimated for 1971 that each life saved is worth $200,000 and each injury avoided is worth $6,000.[5] The former figure is, in fact, fairly close to an estimate by Rosen and Thaler, who measure the value of life by the wage premium required to attract workers to risky jobs.[6] Thus, according to the NHTSA figures, the saving in life and injury costs amounts to $386,000. The National Safety Council estimates that the average 1972 property-damage accident costs $385, so 259 fewer accidents means a saving of around $100,000 in repair bills. The sum of these savings—close to $500,000—fails to offset even half the costs. The clear implications are that lowered speed limits are hardly a worthwhile policy and, indeed, that it would pay to raise existing limits.

The larger implication may be that the case for legal intervention to improve highway safety rests on unsubstantial ground. It should not be surprising that even the most effective intervention, the speed limit, fails to pay its costs. Both the benefits and costs of speed fall largely on the driver, and since, but for the legal costs, he would drive faster, the likely outcome of a cost-benefit analysis of speed limits is not difficult to guess. However, the typical driver may not bear *all* the costs of his speed. The

---

[5] U.S. National Highway Traffic Safety Administration, *Societal Costs of Motor Vehicle Accidents, Preliminary Report* (Washington, D. C.: U.S. Government Printing Office, 1972).

[6] Sherwin Rosen and Richard Thaler, "The Value of Life," mimeographed (University of Rochester, Department of Economics, 1973).
  This practice turns out to imply a value of life of $176,000, in the sense that 1,000 workers would each accept a pay cut of $176 per year to work at a job in which one less member of the group was killed on the job each year.

absence of any speed limit might well induce him to drive too fast, inasmuch as the benefits of speed to him would pay *his* costs of speeding but not *all* the costs of speeding. It is precisely this sort of possibility that exacerbates the inefficiency of regulation of vehicle design. That sort of regulation increases the net benefits of riskier driving to the driver, and if, moreover, he can escape some of the costs that his recklessness imposes on others, his incentive to take greater risk is heightened.

If the divergence between the driver's cost and the total cost of his risky driving strengthens the case against design regulation, it does not immediately strengthen the case for a speed limit. For one thing, why is the driver able to escape some of the costs? For another, are there more efficient devices than a speed limit to induce lower driving speeds? The most obvious reason that a driver escapes some costs is the failure to hold him liable for damage inflicted on others, and the most obvious remedy would be more rigorous and certain enforcement of the liability. Such enforcement is not costless, however, and this is the rationale for something like a speed limit—or, more generally, a tax on driving speed: speed laws, or a set of laws designed to place explicit limits on the accident risk run by drivers, become the method of choice if the cost of administering them is lower than that of imposing full liability for accident costs on drivers.

If it turns out that the cost of administering the court and insurance systems is high enough to recommend legal restraints on driver behavior, the best way to administer those restraints remains a problem. It is hardly clear that existing speed restraints, for example, ought to be as restrictive as they are, and it is less clear that their efficiency has increased over time. For example, the costs and benefits of various driving speeds will vary by locality and according to the value of driving time and to the risk and cost of accidents for specific traffic conditions. The recently enacted national maximum speed limit must necessarily fail to reflect this local variety. Even before it was imposed, local laws were failing to adjust to changed circumstances. The long-run downward trends in the rates of death, injury, and property damage, coupled with a long-run upward trend in the value of time, imply that speed restraints should diminish over time. Indeed, they generally did up to 1960, but after that little change took place until the reduction required by Congress in 1974. (The one mitigating circumstance was the spread of the Interstate Highway System with its high speed limits.)

It is clearly beyond the scope of this study to discuss the optimum configuration of speed restraints, let alone the host of possible alternative or supplementary restraints (driving-age limits, drunk-driving restrictions, and so on). However, even a cursory examination casts doubt on the assumption that these restraints are more soundly based than the regulation of vehicle design.

APPENDIX A: ESTIMATES OF EXPECTED REDUCTION IN DEATH RATE OF VEHICLE OCCUPANTS DUE TO SAFETY DEVICES

This appendix describes the method for deriving the expected reduction in occupant death rates due to selected safety devices, reported in Table 1. The studies used to construct the estimates assume complete installation and use of safety devices. Because part of the 1972 car stock was lacking some or all of these devices, a first step in estimating the reduction is to establish more realistic estimates of the fraction equipped with each device. These estimates, based on the age distribution of the 1972 car stock, are summarized below: [1]

Device	Year Device Became Standard	Implied 1972 Installation Rate
Lap seatbelt	1964	0.95
Energy-absorbing steering column	1967 (except Ford, 1968)	0.56
Shoulder belt	1968	0.49
High-penetration-resistant windshield	1967	0.58
Padded instrument panel	1968	0.49
Dual braking system	1967	0.58

Using these fractions, I derived the estimates in Table 1 in the manner outlined in the following sections.

---

[1] The source of this data is R. L. Polk and Company, *Passenger Cars*, various years, except for data on the lap seatbelt, which is from National Safety Council (hereafter NSC), *Accident Facts*, 1973.

Lap Seatbelt. In its reports for 1969–1972, the National Safety Council (NSC) estimates that available seatbelts are used 40 percent of the time.[2] Given the 1972 installation rate, I take this to imply that they are in use in 38 percent of accidents, and apply this factor to the results of various safety studies.

The National Safety Council estimates that full usage would save 8,000 to 10,000 lives annually.[3] The implicit actual saving (3,000 to 3,800 lives) is roughly 7 to 8.5 percent of the sum of 1972 occupant deaths and the implicit saving.

Huelke and Gikas estimate that full usage would prevent 40 percent of passenger-car deaths (which accounted for 86 percent of all 1972 deaths of vehicle occupants, including those of trucks and buses).[4] I assume that seatbelts prevent no non-auto deaths though they have been standard in most trucks since 1966.

Kihlberg estimates that unbelted occupants are twice as likely to be killed on rural roads as belted drivers.[5] Given the 1972 usage rate for belts, this estimate implies a 19 percent reduction in rural deaths, which accounted for 79 percent of all occupant deaths in 1972. I assume that no lives are saved by belts in urban accidents.

The National Highway Traffic Safety Administration (NHTSA) reports Florida and Nebraska data that imply a 56 percent higher probability of death to unbelted occupants.[6] I applied this probability to all U.S. occupant deaths.

Data from the Cornell Aeronautical Laboratory indicate a 37.3 percent reduction in the death rate with full utilization of lap belts.[7]

Making a survey of other studies (including the Huelke and Gikas study cited in note 4 of this appendix), Joksch and Wuerdeman present "consensus" estimates of the productivity of various

[2] NSC, *Accident Facts*, 1969-1972.

[3] Ibid., various years.

[4] Huelke and Gikas, "Causes of Deaths," pp. 1100-1107.

[5] J. K. Kihlberg, *Efficacy of Seatbelts in Injury and Noninjury Crashes in Rural Utah* (Buffalo: Cornell Aeronautical Laboratory, 1969).

[6] U.S. National Highway Traffic Safety Administration (hereafter NHTSA), *Second Annual Report on the Administration of the National Traffic and Motor Vehicle Safety Act* (Washington, D.C.: U.S. Government Printing Office, 1968).

[7] U.S. Office of Science and Technology, *Cumulative Regulatory Effects on the Cost of Automotive Transportation (RECAT)* (Washington, D.C.: U.S. Government Printing Office, 1972).

devices adjusted for any interaction with other devices.[8] The estimated reduction in the death rate for full utilization of lap belts is 35 percent.

Analyzing data from North Carolina accidents, Levine and Campbell estimated the reduction in the probability of serious injury—a fatal injury or one requiring the victim to be carried from the accident scene—at 43 percent.[9] I assume that this figure applies to fatalities.

Energy-Absorbing Steering Column. Lave and Weber [10] cite data in Huelke and Gikas [11] implying that 5,700, or 15 percent, of 1965 occupant deaths were due to impact with the steering column. From an examination of photographs of twenty-eight such victims, they estimate that half would have survived if the steering column had collapsed (net of those saved by seatbelts), which suggests a reduction of 7.5 percent in the death rate if the device is installed in all cars.

Nahum and Siegel report that energy-absorbing columns prevent all deaths from impact with steering columns at accident speeds up to 50 miles per hour.[12] They make no estimates for speeds greater than 60 miles per hour, but only about 35 percent of fatal accidents in 1965 occurred beyond that speed.[13] I assume that none of the higher-speed deaths is prevented by the device, and apply the implicit 65 percent reduction in total deaths from impact with the steering column to the data in Lave and Weber.[14]

Joksch and Wuerdeman estimate that the energy-absorbing column reduces the probability of a fatality by 0.10.[15]

Levine and Campbell estimate a reduction of 0.142 in the probability of serious injury (see the section on lap seatbelts above) due to the energy-absorbing column. I assume that this figure applies to the fatality subcategory.

---

[8] H.C. Joksch and H. Wuerdeman, "Estimating the Effects of Crash Phase Injury Countermeasures," *Accident Analysis and Prevention,* vol. 4 (June 1972), pp. 89-108.

[9] Levine and Campbell, "Effectiveness of Lap Seatbelts."

[10] Lave and Weber, "Benefit-Cost Analysis," pp. 265-275.

[11] Huelke and Gikas, "Causes of Deaths."

[12] Statement by Allan Nahum and Arnold Siegel, University of California, Los Angeles, before U.S. Senate Commerce Committee, 25 April 1968, cited in NHTSA, *Second Annual Report,* pp. 18-20.

[13] NSC, *Accident Facts,* 1966.

[14] Lave and Weber, "Benefit-Cost Analysis."

[15] Joksch and Wuerdeman, "Estimating the Effects."

For each of the four estimates, I assume that the energy-absorbing column saves only the lives of occupants of passenger cars, though some trucks have similar devices.

Shoulder Belt. In *Accident Facts* for 1972, the National Safety Council reports that, where they are available, shoulder belts are worn less than 10 percent of the time, while the Office of Science and Technology cites a Department of Transportation estimate of 4 percent.[16] I use the lower figure and the 1972 installation rate to estimate that shoulder belts are worn in about 2 percent of accidents, and then apply this estimate to the following results of safety studies.

Bohlin compares the accident-survival experience of drivers of Volvo automobiles, all of which were equipped with a combined lap and shoulder belt.[17] Belted drivers perished only 10 percent as frequently as unbelted drivers. This implies a marginal reduction of 50 percent of occupant deaths through use of shoulder belts, assuming full utilization, and a 40 percent reduction in the death rate from use of lap belts alone.

The marginal reduction of occupant deaths from shoulder belts over what would occur with lap belts is put at 13 percent by Huelke and Gikas;[18] at 16.4 percent by the Office of Science and Technology;[19] and 10 percent by Joksch and Wuerdeman.[20]

High-Penetration-Resistant (HPR) Windshield. Nahum and Siegel report that penetration of the windshield caused death only at accident speeds of 20 to 30 miles per hour, and then in only 4 percent of accidents in which penetration occurred.[21] These deaths were eliminated by the HPR windshield. The NSC's *Accident Facts* for 1966 reported that 13 percent of 1964 fatal accidents occurred at 20 to 30 miles per hour. Only if one assumes that all the fatalities were due to windshield penetration would the Nahum and Siegel data and the HPR windshield installation rate imply a reduction of as much as 0.25 percent in the occupant death rate.

---

[16] Office of Science and Technology, *RECAT*.

[17] N. Bohlin, "A Statistical Analysis of 28,000 Accident Cases with Emphasis on Occupant Restraint Value," in *Proceedings of the 11th Stapp Car Crash Conference* (New York: Society of Automotive Engineers, 1967).

[18] Huelke and Gikas, "Causes of Deaths."

[19] Office of Science and Technology, *RECAT*.

[20] Joksch and Wuerdeman, "Estimating the Effects."

[21] Nahum and Siegel Statement.

According to Joksch and Wuerdeman, full installation of the HPR windshield would reduce fatalities 5 percent for unbelted occupants and 3 percent for belted occupants (because more unbelted occupants strike the windshield).[22] I then assume a propensity of 0.4 to use seatbelts in cars with HPR windshields, which, together with the HPR installation rate, yields the figure in Table 1.

Padded Instrument Panel and Dual Braking System. Lave and Weber conclude that the padded panel does not reduce fatalities at all; they estimate that dual braking would eliminate all deaths due to brake failure, and put these at about 1 percent of occupant fatalities in 1965.[23] I assume that no deaths to pedestrians are caused by brake failure.

APPENDIX B: ESTIMATES OF THE DETERMINANTS OF ACCIDENTS AND ACCIDENT RATES, AND SOURCES OF DATA

The basic model that I seek to estimate may be written as

$$R = f(P, Y, T, A, S, K, u), \tag{B.1}$$

where

R = an accident rate per vehicle mile (this will be defined for accidents of differing severity and for all those affected as well as for motor-vehicle occupants only);

P = the part of the cost of an accident that is ordinarily covered by insurance;

Y = income;

T = secular trend, to account for long-run adjustments;

A = alcoholic intoxication among the population at risk;

S = driving speed;

K = driver age;

u = random factors.

This appendix presents estimates of (B.1) for the period before federal regulation of vehicle design and uses these estimates to project, for the subsequent period, the rates that could have been

---

[22] Joksch and Wuerdeman, "Estimating the Effects."
[23] Lave and Weber, "Benefit-Cost Analysis."

expected without regulation. The effects of regulation are then inferred by a comparison of these expected rates with actual rates.

I developed empirical counterparts to the variables in (B.1) for each year from 1947 through 1972. The initial year was chosen to eliminate most of the effects of adjustment from wartime to peacetime driving conditions. Prewar data are unavailable for some of the series. I assume that 1965 is the last year that vehicle design was unregulated. This predates the formal imposition of safety standards, and treats the sudden ubiquity of lap seatbelts in new cars beginning in 1964 as the de facto result of federal regulation. (An extra year is allowed for measurable effects of this development to show up in the car stock.)

The time series used to estimate equation (B.1) are given here: Accident rates, R, represent some measure of damage divided by vehicle miles driven. The specific numerators employed for each are as follows:

TDR is the total death rate—all motor vehicle deaths in the United States in the year.[1]

VDR is the vehicle-occupant death rate—total motor-vehicle deaths less deaths to pedestrians, bicyclists, and motorcyclists. (Motorcycles are not treated as "vehicles" because the safety standards of concern here do not apply to them and their accident rates are atypical of those for more conventional vehicles.) Pedestrian deaths typically account for over 80 percent of deaths to nonvehicle occupants.[2]

TIR is the total injury rate—total nonfatal injuries due to motor vehicle accidents.[3]

VIR is the vehicle occupant injury rate—total nonfatal injuries less those to pedestrians and bicyclists.[4]

PDR and PIR are nonoccupant death and injury rates, respectively; each represents differences between the appropriate total and occupant rates.

$DMGR$ is the property-damage rate—the number of vehicles involved in accidents resulting only in property damage.[5]

---

[1] For data for 1947-1950, see NSC, *Accident Facts*, 1973; for 1951-1972, see NHTSA, *A Report on Activities under the National Traffic and Motor Vehicle Safety Act* (Washington, D.C.: U.S. Government Printing Office, 1973).

[2] Ibid.

[3] NSC, *Accident Facts*, various years.

[4] Ibid. Separate data for motorcyclists are not reported.

[5] Ibid.

Most of the empirical work is based on rates standardized for type of driving (urban or rural) and type of road (four-lane limited-access or other), which are prefixed "A"—for example, *ATDR*. This standardization was adopted because of the potential inaccuracy from impounding all omitted variables into a trend term. Accident rates differ widely by area (death rates are higher and injury and damage rates lower in rural areas), but there is no clear trend in the urban-rural composition of driving. To remove the influence of shifts in this composition (and conserve a valuable degree of freedom), the adjusted rates are simple averages of urban and rural rates (because the postwar averages of urban and rural vehicle miles are roughly equal). Similarly, accident rates are much lower on multi-lane limited-access roads than on other roads (ranging from roughly half for death rates down to a tenth for accident rates). Differences among other types of roads are comparatively trivial. However, the safety benefits of limited-access roads are poorly represented by the linear trend. Only with the substantial construction of the Interstate Highway System in the 1960s does the proportion of total vehicle miles driven on such roads assume any importance. This bunching suggests that a linear-trend model would be better applied to death rates on more conventional roads.[6] Such rates are available only for a few recent years, but estimates can be derived for all years for both urban and rural driving. These estimates are employed in the adjusted accident rates.[7]

---

[6] This suggestion would imply, however, that any gradual improvement in conventional highways was not neglected when the interstate roads were built.

[7] The estimates are derived as follows: For the years from 1967 to 1971, death and injury rates, as well as vehicle miles and highway miles on interstate and other highways, are available in U.S. Federal Highway Administration (hereafter FHA), *Fatal and Injury Accident Rates* (Washington, D.C.: U.S. Government Printing Office, various years). In any year, the relevant adjusted accident rate (*AR*) for urban or rural driving is related to the overall rate (*R*) as follows:

$$AR = \frac{R \cdot TVM}{k \cdot LVM + OVM},$$

where

    TVM = vehicle miles driven on all roads
    LVM = vehicle miles on limited access roads
    $OVM = TVM - LVM$
    k = ratio of the rate on limited-access roads to the rate on other roads.

Since k is unavailable prior to 1967, I used the average 1967-1971 ratio as an estimate for all years. To make the necessary estimates for the components of *TVM*, I assumed that the ratio of travel density (*VM* per highway mile) on

The cost of an accident, P, includes two major components that are generally covered by insurance—bodily injury and property damage. Given my assumption that a driver can "buy" an accident only at the cost of paying his insurance company some proportion of these and associated administrative costs engendered by the accident, I express P as an index of these costs. Specifically, P is a weighted average of the consumer price indexes for physician and hospital costs and for auto-repair services deflated by the overall CPI and multiplied by an insurance loading charge. The weights are the proportions of the insurance-premium dollar spent on bodily injury insurance (0.4) and property-damage insurance (0.6) over the sample period. The actual insurance loading charge—the ratio of premiums to benefits—is known only ex post, while the expected load should be relevant to the driver's decision. Instead of assuming that drivers have perfect foresight,

limited-access highways to that on all highways in any year equals the average 1967-1971 ratio for interstate and all roads. Separate ratios were calculated for urban and rural roads (and neither showed any obvious trend for 1967-1971). The resulting estimate of the limited-access density in any year (the 1967-1971 density ratio times the all-road density in that year) was multiplied by the mileage on limited-access highways to obtain LVM, and by subtraction, OVM.

Unfortunately, complete data on highway mileage are unavailable, since they are reported by partly overlapping political jurisdictions (state primary systems, Interstate Highway System, and Federal Aid System). For example, a city freeway may be part of the Federal Aid System but of neither of the other two, while a toll road may be part of the last two but not the first. I used the mileage on state primary limited-access roads, since this is usually the largest total. The excluded mileage is bound to be trivial, given the dominant role of the Interstate Highway System, almost all of which is in state primary systems. The data are available from 1956, when such roads covered only about 1,000 miles, compared with over 30,000 currently. I assumed arbitrarily that 600 such miles existed at the end of World War II and that the figure increased linearly to 1956. Any reasonable alternative assumption would affect the results trivially.

The values of k applied to the resulting LVM series are 0.59 and 0.49 for urban and rural death rates, respectively, and 0.30 and 0.36 for injury rates. The FHA does not report property-damage experience. However, National Safety Council data on several turnpikes for 1965 and 1966, reported in the 1966 and 1967 editions of *Accident Facts*, showed that property-damage accidents occurred twice as frequently as injury accidents on these roads, but ten times as frequently as on all roads. This implies a k for property-damage accidents one-fifth the 0.34 urban-rural average for injury accidents; I rounded this to 0.07. (By a similar procedure, the implicit k for property damage is about one-eighth the 0.54 average for death, or also about 0.07.)

In general, the road-specific accident rates and the crude rates were virtually identical through about 1960 and then diverged gradually though unevenly. By 1965, the two were something like 5 percent apart for deaths and injuries, and the difference widened to 10 percent by 1971. The corresponding figures for property damage are double these.

I constructed a crude approximation to the expected loading charge by dividing this year's premiums by last year's benefit payments. The assumption here is that insurance is bought at the start of the year, at which time both magnitudes are known.[8]

Income, Y, is defined here as real earned income per adult of working age (fifteen and over).[9] This figure was chosen after a preliminary investigation of several alternatives, discussed below. Earned income is estimated disposable personal income from wages, salaries, business proprietorships, and farms (thus it excludes transfers, rents, dividends, and interest).[10]

A linear trend is represented by T.

Alcoholic intoxication, A, is measured by consumption of distilled spirits per person fifteen and older. The measure excludes illegal consumption, which has been estimated at around 15 percent of the total.[11]

Vehicle speed, S, is the estimated average speed of motor vehicles on non-interstate rural roads at off-peak hours.[12] Similar data for urban roads are too sparse to be useful.

---

[8] For price indexes, see U.S. Bureau of Labor Statistics, Consumer Price Index (Washington, D.C.: U.S. Government Printing Office), various issues; for automobile insurance premiums and benefits for 1947-1965, see U.S. Bureau of the Census, Statistical Abstract of the United States (Washington, D. C.: U.S. Government Printing Office, various years), and for 1966-1969, Spectator Company, Property Liability Insurance Review (Philadelphia: Spectator Co.), various issues.

[9] See U.S. Department of Commerce, National Income and Product Accounts, 1929-65 (Washington, D.C.: U.S. Government Printing Office, 1966), and Survey of Current Business, various issues.

[10] Ibid. For purposes of the estimate, personal tax payments were assumed to represent the same percentage of each source of income in any year as total personal tax liabilities represented of total personal income less transfer payments for that year. Nominal income was deflated by the deflator for disposable personal income.

[11] Gavin-Jobson Co., The Liquor Handbook, 1973 (New York: Gavin-Jobson Co., 1974).

[12] Statistical Abstract of the United States, various years, and FHA, "Traffic Speed Trends," press release, various issues. The available data for 1961 to 1969, from the FHA press releases "Traffic Speed Trends," are for interstate roads (s_i) and all roads (s_t). The estimate for non-limited-access highways (s_n) is the solution to

$$s_t = \left(1 - \frac{LVM}{TVM}\right)s_n + \left(\frac{LVM}{TVM}\right)s_i$$

for the single unknown; TVM is rural vehicle miles and LVM is rural vehicle miles on state primary limited-access multi-lane highways. For years before 1961, the 1961 ratio (s_n/s_i) is assumed to prevail. The post-1969 data are spliced to the estimated s_n series.

The number of young drivers, K, is measured by a proxy, the ratio of the population fifteen to twenty-five years old to those older.[13]

Death Rates. Table B-1 contains estimates of equation (B.1) for death rates, using earned income per adult as the income concept. Preliminary work with alternative concepts made it clear that the forces producing a positive relationship between income and the death rate consistently dominated short-run behavior. Every definition of income employed had a positive partial correlation with death rates and was coupled with a strong negative trend effect. Apparently, much of this short-run behavior is consistent with driver response to changes in the shadow price of leisure. While the speed variable may pick up part of this response, it must miss most commuting traffic and will not capture all risks induced by a rise in the price of leisure (such as the risk attending more frequent passing of other cars). In consequence, as work-time components come more to dominate the definition of income, its coefficient tends to become more accurate and the explanatory power of the regression increases. Specifically, for the *ATDR* regression, the following results were obtained:

Definition of income	t-ratio of income coefficient	Standard error of regression estimate (x 100)
Per capita permanent income	2.73	1.90
Per capita personal consumption expenditures (proxy for permanent income)	3.26	1.84
Per capita disposable personal income	3.64	1.75
Disposable personal income per working-age adult	3.73	1.72
Earned income per working-age adult (Table B-1 concept)	4.32	1.59

[13] *Statistical Abstract of the United States*, various years. Accurate distributions of driver age are available for only a few years.

Table B-1

REGRESSION ESTIMATES, DEATH RATES, 1947–1965 [a]

Dependent Variables [b]	Independent Variables						Summary Statistic		
	P	Y	T	A	S	K	R^2 [d]	SE × 100 [e]	DW [f]
ATDR	−0.172	0.884	−0.074	0.359	1.843	0.827	0.994	1.585	2.080
	(−1.792)	(4.317)	(−13.900)	(2.591)	(3.863)	(12.232)			
AVDR	−0.045	0.906	−0.068	0.451	2.301	0.594	0.978	1.987	1.725
	(−0.370)	(3.528)	(−10.073)	(2.592)	(3.847)	(7.002)			
APDR	−0.432	0.735	−0.092	0.112	1.016	1.274	0.995	2.658	2.247
	(−2.680)	(2.140)	(10.185)	(0.481)	(1.271)	(11.234)			

[a] The numbers in parentheses are t-ratios.

[b] Since, in natural units, $ATDR = AVDR + APDR$, the predicted values of one regression should be, but are not, constrained by those of the other two. However, there is almost perfect correlation (around 0.99) between the constrained and unconstrained predicted values for each series.

[c] All variables except T are in natural logarithms. The regression constant is deleted.

[d] R^2 = coefficient of determination.

[e] SE = standard error of estimate.

[f] DW = Durbin-Watson statistic. (None implies significant autocorrelation of residuals.)

Source: See text for sources, description of series and definitions of variables.

The limited degrees of freedom available made experimentation with much more refined concepts impractical. For example, the definition used in Table B-1 implicitly assumes a zero price of leisure for those unemployed or out of the labor force, and does not distinguish permanent from transitory effects. Nevertheless, the results seem generally consistent with a regime in which the cheapest immediate response to an unexpected increase in income is to increase driving intensity, especially where failure to do so entails a sacrifice of income-earning opportunities. (The presumption here is that deviations of income from trend are unexpected.) The strong negative trend effect can then be interpreted as reflecting, in part, a longer-run response to changes in permanent income, whereby adjustments of such factors as vehicle design are made in order to reduce the costs entailed by permanently increased driving intensity. A rationale for such a temporal pattern might be that the cost-benefit ratio of making an immediate conversion of a major part of the existing vehicle stock and highway mileage to a safer design is greater than the cost-benefit ratio of driving the existing stock more intensively.

If the trend term is a partial proxy for permanent income, the regressions seem to imply that the net effect of a (permanent) increase in income is to reduce death rates;[14] that is, the average contribution to death rates from the income term in the regressions is on the order of +2 percent annually and is more than offset by the trend effect. (Part of that offset need not be connected with lagged income effects.)[15]

---

[14] In cross-section regressions, discussed in Peltzman, "Effect of Safety Regulation," I found that the income effect on state death rates was consistently and strongly negative. The income elasticity was on the order of -1. Since state income differences tend to persist, the cross-section evidence is consistent with a net long-run negative income effect.

[15] The behavior of the various income time series reflects a pro-cyclical pattern of trend-adjusted death rates that cannot be rationalized completely on value-of-time grounds. The residuals from the Table B-1 regressions tend to be highest and lowest at cyclical peaks and troughs respectively. Attempts to gain further insight into this cyclical behavior proved unrewarding. Specifically, I examined the following:

Travel density. The regressions implicitly assume unit elasticity of deaths with respect to vehicle miles. The probability of accident per vehicle mile may increase with density (vehicle miles per highway mile), which may in turn behave pro-cyclically. However, when density was added to the ATDR regression, its coefficient was insignificant, though positive.

New cars. It has been suggested (see *Wall Street Journal,* 22 January 1974) that increased risk of deaths is a cost of driver familiarization with new cars, sales of which are pro-cyclical. However, the ratio of new cars to the total car stock had an insignificant negative coefficient when added to the ATDR regression. One would like to generalize the argument by

The remaining regression coefficients in Table B-1 (all of which are elasticities) consistently have the predicted signs, and are typically significant. The one important exception is the price coefficient, which is significant only for pedestrian deaths. Alcohol, speed, and youth also appear to contribute differently to occupant and pedestrian deaths. In the case of the first two, their greater elasticity with respect to occupant deaths is consistent with the highway-safety literature. However, the (significant) difference between the driver-age elasticities is surprising. The vehicle-occupant elasticity corresponds closely with the crude difference in death rates among age groups, but the much larger pedestrian elasticity implies that young drivers are peculiarly prone to impose risks on pedestrians.

The striking size of the speed elasticities should be interpreted cautiously. Taken literally, they would attribute about 40 percent of all current highway deaths to the postwar increase in vehicle speed—over and above the speed effect implicit in the positive income elasticity.[16] However, the temporal adjustment process at work with income may also operate with respect to speed; that is, greater speed may be the most efficient immediate response to increased demand for risky driving, while the loss-prevention expenditures induced by this demand are spread over time and are therefore reflected in the trend coefficient.

The Effects of Safety Devices on Death Rates. I use the regressions in Table B-1 and post-1965 values of the independent variables to generate predictions of death rates for recent years. These are shown in Table B-2. If the evidence from safety studies is taken at face value, the projected rates should exceed the actual rates

---

examining the response for new drivers, but the required data are unavailable.

Error in measuring vehicle miles. A spurious pro-cyclical death rate would be produced if the FHA estimate of vehicle miles were smoother than the actual series. However, residuals from a regression of vehicle miles on gasoline consumption were uncorrelated with cycles in income.

Driver age. If access of young drivers to the family car is correlated with income, the high accident risk of these drivers will contribute to a pro-cyclical death rate. However, the population death rate for all age categories behaves pro-cyclically. The cycles are slightly more pronounced for those aged fifteen to twenty-five, but this is hardly sufficient to account for much of the cyclical nature of the total death rate.

[16] That is, S will be imperfectly correlated with work-related driving speed, because it specifically measures speeds at off-peak hours. I assumed that independent variation in work-related speed is correlated with the shadow price of leisure.

by continually widening amounts until in 1972 a gap between them of perhaps 20 percent would be attained. However, no such gap is evident in the behavior of the total death rate (ATDR). Indeed, the projected ATDR tracks the actual rate to within 2 percent up to 1972, when it falls below the actual by 5 percent. While this last difference hints at a perverse effect of safety regulation, the standard error of the 1972 regression forecast is too large to permit acceptance of this hint. Virtually identical results were obtained by substituting the unadjusted TDR for ATDR in these calculations (the 1972 TDR exceeds its projected value by 4.1 percent). Finally, I estimated the ATDR regression on 1947–1972 data, adding the fraction of the car stock of 1964 and later vintage (that is, the vintage subject to federal safety regulation); these results are reported in line 1972A. The coefficient of this variable yields an estimate of the productivity of regulation which should be biased upward.[17] However, the bias is too small to alter the basic conclusion: the 1972 effect and the t-ratio of the coefficient of the pseudo-proxy for safety regulation are reported on line 1972A of Table B-2, and both are of no importance. The implication of all this is that essentially nothing in the post-1965 behavior of the total death rate can corroborate that safety devices provide the kind of lifesaving suggested in the safety literature (or, indeed, any lifesaving at all). This behavior can in fact be explained entirely by the forces that explain variation in the death rate before these devices became mandatory.[18]

---

[17] The regression constrains the pre- and post-regulatory coefficients to be equal. However, this is not to be the case generally. Suppose, for example, that every increase in income induces a greater increase in driving intensity when the safety devices are mandatory than it does when they are not. In that case, the direct effect of safety regulation as estimated by the coefficient may be favorable, but the effect would be offset by that of higher income. A similar argument would apply if safety regulation were simply a particular manifestation of an income effect. The implication of this argument and analogous ones shows up in the expanded regression: it has a larger income and driver-age elasticity and a smaller price elasticity than the Table B-1 counterparts. However, the alcohol elasticities are roughly equal, and the speed elasticity is lower in the expanded regression. This last result implies that the mandatory safety devices are particularly effective in protecting against the effects of high-speed accidents, though the increased income coefficient casts some doubt on this implication.

On a similar argument, projection of death rates from preregulation parameters may overstate the productivity of regulation. If regulation induces an increase in speed, for example, the projected death rate will be higher than in a pure "no-regulation" world.

[18] I am told, by representatives of domestic auto manufacturers, that my results may also reflect failure to account for effects of the recent increase in sales of imports. Most studies show that the probability of death in an

Table B-2
ACTUAL AND PROJECTED DEATH RATES,[a] 1966-1972

Year	Adjusted Total Death Rate				Adjusted Vehicle-Occupant Death Rate				Adjusted Pedestrian Death Rate			
	Actual	Pro-jected	DIFF [b]	T [c]	Actual	Pro-jected	DIFF [b]	T [c]	Actual	Pro-jected	DIFF [b]	T [c]
1965	5.83	5.87	-0.6	—	4.54	4.58	-0.6	0	1.29	1.30	-0.6	—
1966	6.04	5.90	2.4	1.04	4.68	4.68	0	0	1.36	1.25	8.4	2.21
1967	5.83	5.75	1.4	0.58	4.51	4.64	-2.8	-0.93	1.32	1.16	12.9	3.15
1968	5.78	5.73	0.9	0.28	4.51	4.75	-5.2	-1.30	1.27	1.09	15.3	2.88
1969	5.67	5.76	-1.6	-0.53	4.49	4.79	-6.5	-1.74	1.18	1.09	7.9	1.58
1970	5.37	5.28	1.7	0.55	4.16	4.36	-4.7	-1.21	1.21	1.00	19.1	3.67
1971	5.11	5.10	0.2	0.05	3.91	4.31	-9.7	-2.12	1.20	0.92	26.6	4.36
1972	5.06	4.83	4.7	0.98	3.86	4.14	-7.0	-1.17	1.20	0.84	35.6	4.45
1972A [d]	5.06	5.08	-0.3	-0.37	3.86	4.24	-9.6	-2.16	1.20	0.93	25.7	2.53

a Projected rates are antilogs of the values obtained by entering 1966-1972 values of the independent variables in the Table B-1 regressions. Rates are expressed in deaths per 100 million vehicle miles. See text for discussion of rates and adjustments.

b This is the difference between actual and projected natural logs of death rate multiplied by 100, so it can be interpreted as a percentage for continuous compounding.

c T is the ratio of DIFF, as defined in note b, to the standard error of forecast from the Table B-1 regression.

d Line 1972A is obtained from 1947-1972 regressions of the same form as those in Table B-1, except for the addition of a variable, the fraction of the vehicle stock of 1964 or later vintage. Here the projected values are obtained by subtracting the 1972 effect of this variable (its coefficient times the 1972 value) from the 1972 predicted value of the regression. DIFF is computed from the difference of the 1972 actual and adjusted-predicted value, and T is the ratio of the coefficient of the car-stock variable to its standard error.

Actual values for 1965 and those predicted by the Table B-1 regressions are shown for comparison with subsequent years.

Source: Regressions in Table B-1, using post-1965 data. See also discussion in text.

Table B-2 also contains data on the distribution of highway deaths among vehicle occupants and pedestrians. These can help distinguish among rival explanations for the overall ineffectuality of safety regulation. If this regulation has not merely ratified market forces, a shift toward nonoccupant deaths should occur, and there is evidence of such a shift in Table B-2. Death rates for occupants do tend to drop further below projected values over time. If the consistent (though sometimes insignificant) over-projection of AVDR and the significant (biased) coefficient of the regulatory variable on line 1972A lead to acceptance of the hypothesis that regulation has saved lives of drivers, then the magnitude involved appears to be on the order of half that suggested by a naïve reading of the safety literature. At the same time, the APDR regression for the period before regulation consistently underprojects death rates after regulation, and these differences are usually significant. The differences are so large that they engender skepticism, but neither adjustment for growth in the number of bicyclists and motorcyclists (who are included with pedestrians) nor use of a death rate based on population rather than vehicle miles changes the basic results.[19]

accident is higher for occupants of small cars, which until recently were predominantly imported cars (and vice versa). However, the essential point of this study is that any such differential probability will induce driver responses working in an opposite direction. When I added the fraction of cars that are imports to the regressions, its effect was insignificant, and some crude post-1965 data tended to confirm this insignificance. Among the major industrial states, California and (as one would expect) Michigan are at opposite extremes in the receptivity of their drivers toward imports. In the former, the share of imports in total registrations was about 20 percent in 1972 and has grown rapidly in recent years. In the latter, the import share is roughly 5 percent and has grown little. (The 1972 U.S. average share is about 10 percent.) However, no parallel divergence is apparent in recent trends in the highway death rate. The 1963-1965 death rates for the two states were virtually identical (5.1 per 100 million miles in California, and 5.3 in Michigan), reflecting a basic similarity of driving characteristics. That similarity has apparently dominated their recent experience, because their 1970-1972 death rates were still virtually identical (3.9 for California and 4.0 for Michigan). One can add Illinois to this group, since its drivers have been only a little less hostile to imports than Michigan's. The Illinois death rate closely tracks that of the other two states, falling from 5.0 to 4.0 in the same period. Thus, something like a controlled experiment leaves little room for attributing the lack of effectiveness of safety regulation to the expansion of imports.

[19] Bicycle and motorcycle deaths were a growing portion of nonoccupant deaths prior to 1965. If it is assumed that the ratio of these deaths to other nonoccupant deaths had maintained its pre-1965 growth rate (about 3 percent annually), and that none of its recent acceleration was due to substitution

Injury and Property Damage. Effective regulation should also mean that accidents have less severe results. In some accidents that otherwise would have caused death, only injury will occur; in others, property damage, rather than injury, will be the worst result. While one cannot predict the net effect on total injuries, pedestrians should bear a larger share of the burden of injuries, just as they do with deaths. And a net increase in accidents involving property damage should be observed.

Regression estimates of equation (B.1) with injury and property damage rates as the dependent variables are presented in Table B-3. These are subject to much more measurement error than are death rates.[20] However, the regressions suspiciously mirror their counterparts in Table B-1, most notably in their lack of residual variance. If there are any notable differences between the two sets, they might be the generally lower income elasticity for the less severe accidents and the larger price elasticity of damage accidents. In view of the close correspondence between the accident series before safety regulation,[21] any great difference in their subsequent behavior would be surprising.

---

for pedestrian deaths, then the 1972 *APDR* would have been about 5 percent lower than it was.

The use of vehicle miles to deflate nonoccupant deaths assumes implicitly that driver action "causes" these deaths. At another extreme, one could assume that pedestrians seek risk independently of driver action, vehicle density, and other such factors. In that case, population, as a proxy for the number of pedestrians seeking risk, would be the more appropriate deflator. But when the figures in Table B-2 are obtained from a regression using a population death rate, the underprojection of post-1965 death rates actually becomes more severe (by about 10 percentage points). One reason is that vehicle miles have an effect on pedestrian deaths, and the growth in this variable has accelerated relative to that in population in recent years. Finally, use of unadjusted death rates reveals the same shift in the incidence of risk as is revealed by the adjusted data. The projected *PDR* is 26 percent below the actual and the projected *VDR* is 5 percent above the actual in 1972.

[20] This difference results from the greater degree of under-reporting and subjectivity of definition involved in less severe accidents. The resulting problems are well illustrated by a comparison of the NSC injury series, which I use here, with an alternative series compiled by the Travelers Insurance Company: the two are not in remote agreement on either the level or the rate of change in motor vehicle injuries. The Travelers estimate of total injuries is currently about two and one-half times that of the NSC, though the immediate postwar excess was only about 30 percent. In recent years, the Federal Highway Administration has also collected injury data, and these data run roughly at the geometric mean of the other two series. The National Safety Council is the sole source of property-accident estimates, but these estimates are bedeviled by sporadically changing reporting requirements, and are consequently rounded generously.

[21] The correlation between any two accident rates is typically above 0.95.

48

Table B-3

REGRESSION ESTIMATES, INJURY AND PROPERTY-DAMAGE RATES, 1947–1965

Dependent Variables	Independent Variables						Summary Statistic		
	P	Y	T	A	S	K	R^2	SE × 100	DW
ATIR	−0.249	0.524	−0.067	0.295	2.224	0.670	0.983	2.190	3.010
	(−1.770)	(1.807)	(−9.203)	(1.524)	(3.473)	(7.050)			
AVIR	−0.220	0.503	−0.064	0.399	2.594	0.469	0.957	2.502	2.882
	(−1.371)	(1.516)	(−7.635)	(1.803)	(3.546)	(4.318)			
APIR	−0.290	0.318	−0.096	−0.322	1.624	1.574	0.993	4.010	1.738
	(−1.128)	(0.598)	(−7.147)	(−0.908)	(1.386)	(9.041)			
ADMGR	−0.515	0.818	−0.069	0.466	1.663	0.527	0.960	2.891	1.473
	(−2.938)	(2.190)	(−7.070)	(1.843)	(1.912)	(4.271)			

Source: See Table B-1 and text.

49

The post-regulatory experience of injury rates does mirror that of death rates. The important exception is injury rates for vehicle occupants. The projections from the $AVIR$ regression in Table B-3 (see Table B-4) are usually below the actual values, though the differences are insignificant. Similarly, the coefficient of the fraction of cars subject to regulation in the expanded form of that regression is insignificant (line 1972A). Therefore, the weak evidence in favor of a reduction in occupant deaths due to regulation does not hold up for injuries. However, there is evidence that regulation worsened the rates of injury to pedestrians by roughly the same magnitudes observed for death rates. But, since the series on vehicle occupants dominates the total, it is not safe to conclude that total injury rates have been adversely affected by regulation.

Table B-4 also compares projected and actual rates for accidents involving property damage. These series behave differently from the series on both the death rate and the injury rate, and in precisely the way one would predict if safety regulation has been at all effective: there were significantly more damage accidents after regulation than could have been expected. Furthermore, the size of the gap is startling. Both of the estimates for 1972 imply an excess of about 4 million damage accidents.[22]

Canadian Accident Data. Canadian data, which classify cars involved in accidents by model year, can be used to test the hypothesis that regulation induces increased driver risk. The focus here will be on the ratio of cars from model year m to all cars reporting involvement in an accident in year t (RA_{mt}). To isolate the impact of regulation on RA, I will take account of the effects of the ratio of cars from m to the total car stock in t (RC_{mt}), and the age of cars from m in t (V_{mt}). The latter variable is included as much to standardize for reporting differences as to measure a true age effect: accidents involving older cars more frequently fail to meet minimum-damage criteria for reporting. The basic regulatory variable (SR_m) uses the information from Table 1 that lap seatbelts account for about 60 percent of the total expected productivity of safety devices. It is defined as zero if m is before 1964, 0.6 for m from 1964–1966, and 1.0 for 1967 and later vintages. The effect of regulation on the share of any one vintage in accidents will be diluted as cars subject to regu-

---

[22] The unadjusted damage rates behave similarly; the actual rate exceeds the projected rate by 0.264 (natural log units) in 1972.

Table B-4
ACTUAL AND PROJECTED INJURY AND PROPERTY-DAMAGE RATES, 1966–1972

Year	Adjusted Total Injury Rate				Adjusted Vehicle-Occupant Injury Rate			
	Actual	Projected	DIFF	T	Actual	Projected	DIFF	T
1965	217	216	0.5		196	195	0.5	
1966	221	215	2.8	0.88	199	196	1.5	0.42
1967	215	209	2.8	0.80	194	192	1.0	0.26
1968	217	206	5.2	1.16	196	192	2.0	0.39
1969	208	210	-1.0	-0.23	188	196	-4.2	-0.88
1970	200	191	4.6	1.05	181	178	1.7	0.34
1971	191	185	3.2	0.62	173	174	-0.6	-0.10
1972	191	173	9.9	1.46	174	163	6.5	0.84
1972A	191	185	3.0	0.15	174	175	-0.5	-0.48

Year	Adjusted Nonoccupant Death Rate				Adjusted Property Damage Rate			
	Actual	Projected	DIFF	T	Actual	Projected	DIFF	T
1965	21	21	0.1		1490	1475	1.0	
1966	22	20	9.6	1.68	1491	1456	2.4	0.59
1967	21	18	12.8	2.10	1466	1414	3.6	0.82
1968	20	17	17.1	2.14	1500	1358	10.0	1.72
1969	20	17	16.1	2.19	1544	1397	10.0	1.85
1970	19	15	21.5	2.76	1535	1285	17.8	3.12
1971	18	14	22.9	2.49	1503	1208	21.8	3.25
1972	17	13	27.8	2.32	1499	1107	30.3	3.48
1972A	17	13	27.0	3.00	1499	1125	28.3	3.071

Source: See Table B-2 and text.

lation become more common, both because of the laws of simple arithmetic [23] and because of the increased probability that pre-regulation cars will be struck by post-regulation models. As the latter approach ubiquity, the effect of regulation on the share of any one vintage in the higher accident total will vanish. To develop a linear approximation to this process, let $B \cdot SR_m$ be the partial effect of regulation on RA_{mt}, where B is a coefficient. However, that coefficient should decline as the fraction of the car stock subject to regulation (FR_t) rises; B can then be expressed as

$$B_0 + B_1 \cdot FR_t ,$$

so that the partial effect of regulation becomes

$$B_0 \cdot SR_m + B_1(SR_m \cdot FR_t) .$$

One would expect $B_0 > 0$, $B_1 < 0$, and, more precisely, $B_0 = |B_1|$ (so that the partial effect vanishes when $FR = 1$).

The results of the regression on Canadian data fulfill these expectations. The regression is

$$RA_{mt} = 6.65 + 0.59RC_{mt} - 0.54V_{mt} + 2.07SR_m - 2.14(SR_m \cdot FR_t) .$$
$$(11.14) \quad (-13.00) \quad (3.24) \quad (-2.15)$$

$$R^2 = 0.92 ; \quad SE = 0.89.$$

Here and in the following equations, the numbers in parentheses are t-ratios and RA and RC are expressed in percentage points. The sample consists of models ten years old and less (which usually account for about 90 percent of the total stock) for the years 1959–1972, or 140 observations,[24] of which 45 are subject to regulation. The interesting result, of course, is that the coefficients of the regulatory and interaction variables have the sign pattern and the (virtual) equality of absolute value that is consistent with a regulation-induced increase in driver risk-taking. The magnitude of the coefficient of SR is also of interest. It im-

---

[23] For example, suppose that the car stock consists of v equal-sized vintages, of which k are regulated. If x is the probability that a car from any of the k will be involved in an accident and y the probability for a pre-regulatory car, RA will be

$$\frac{x}{kx + (v - k)y} .$$

This will be $1/v$ if x and y are equal, but it must approach $1/v$ as k approaches v even if x exceeds y.

[24] In some cases, the original accident data were for groups of vintages. For these, I allocated the group total among vintages in proportion to the vintage share of cars. This procedure therefore biases the coefficient of RC toward unity and overstates its accuracy.

plies that if the average vintage in the sample (8.75 percent of the car stock and 9 percent of accidents) is made subject to regulation, its accident frequency increases fully 25 percent. This increase is sufficient to offset the reduction in deaths per accident claimed by the safety literature for required safety devices, and it is well within the range of my estimate that regulation has induced an excess frequency of accidents of around 30 percent for the United States.

The Effect of Regulation on Driving Speed. To examine the effect of regulation on driving speed, I first estimate the following regression on pre-regulation data (1947–1965):

$$S = \text{Constant} + 0.013T + 0.109Y - 0.210PG - 1.311IM\,.$$
$$\qquad\qquad\quad (4.535) \quad (1.262) \quad (-2.819) \quad (-2.618)$$

$$R^2 = 0.988; \text{SE} = 0.75 \times 10^2; \text{DW} = 2.327\,.$$

Here, in addition to symbols defined previously, PG = log of the consumer price index for gasoline, divided by the overall CPI (gas consumption per mile increases with vehicle speed), and IM = ratio of imports to the total stock of cars (imports typically have lower speed capability than domestic cars). I then project values of S for the post-regulation period, 1966–1972, from this regression to see whether they fall short of the actual values. In fact, the projected and actual values are consistently within 1 or 2 percent of each other, so the hypothesis of a regulation-induced increase in vehicle speed must be rejected. The same result is obtained by adding the fraction of cars subject to regulation to a regression on 1947–1972 data. The coefficient of the variable is less than a tenth its standard error.